TO:

FROM:

GW00494618

I THOUGHT GROWING OLD WOULD TAKE LONGER

*Compiled by the ageless editors
of Peter Pauper Press*

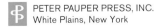

PETER PAUPER PRESS, INC.
White Plains, New York

*To you, who got to see
all the cool bands*

Designed by Margaret Rubiano
Images used under license from Shutterstock.com

Copyright © 2019
Peter Pauper Press, Inc.
202 Mamaroneck Avenue
White Plains, NY 10601 USA
All rights reserved
ISBN 978-1-4413-3134-2
Printed in China

7 6 5 4 3 2 1

I THOUGHT GROWING OLD WOULD TAKE LONGER

IT TAKES A LONG WHILE TO GROW YOUNG.

PABLO PICASSO

A toast to the glory years, when the long strange trip of life offers up a view. The challenges of younger years, with their emotional storms and stressful strivings, have given way to a curious freedom to just be. And if just being entails a certain amount of attitude, so be it. Time to live your life and forget your age, but hang onto that moral high ground that aging brings—a certain gravitas that belies the fact that we're still young at heart, still curious, still learning, and still kicking ass.

AGING IS AN EXTRAORDINARY PROCESS WHERE YOU BECOME THE PERSON YOU ALWAYS SHOULD HAVE BEEN.

DAVID BOWIE

WE DON'T GET
SMARTER AS
WE GET OLDER.
WE JUST RUN OUT OF
STUPID THINGS
TO DO.

LIFE IS SHORT. IF YOU DOUBT ME, ASK A BUTTERFLY. THEIR AVERAGE LIFE SPAN IS A MERE FIVE TO FOURTEEN DAYS.

ELLEN DEGENERES

MAY YOU LIVE
TO BE SO OLD
THAT YOUR
DRIVING
TERRIFIES
PEOPLE.

AGE GETS BETTER WITH WINE.

YOU KNOW YOU'RE GETTING OLD WHEN YOU GET THAT ONE CANDLE ON THE CAKE. IT'S LIKE, "SEE IF YOU CAN BLOW *THIS* OUT."

JERRY SEINFELD

I'VE REACHED THAT AGE WHERE MY BRAIN WENT FROM "YOU PROBABLY SHOULDN'T SAY THAT" TO "WHAT THE HELL, LET'S SEE WHAT HAPPENS."

WE'RE ALL MATURE
UNTIL SOMEONE
PULLS OUT
BUBBLE WRAP.

AGING GRACEFULLY IS AN ART. AGING DISGRACEFULLY IS A TOTAL BLAST.

A GREAT PLEASURE IN LIFE IS DOING WHAT PEOPLE SAY YOU CANNOT DO.

WALTER BAGEHOT

THE BIGGEST LIE
I TELL MYSELF IS,
"I DON'T NEED
TO WRITE THAT
DOWN. I'LL
REMEMBER IT."

YOU KNOW
YOU'RE GETTING
OLD WHEN
ALL YOUR
FAVORITE
DRUGS ARE
LEGAL.

DON'T LET AGING GET YOU DOWN. IT'S TOO HARD TO GET BACK UP!

IF YOU'RE 65
YEARS OLD ON
EARTH, YOU'D BE
ONLY ABOUT 35
ON MARS. YOU'RE
NOT GETTING OLD;
YOU'RE JUST ON
THE WRONG
PLANET.

I MAY BE OLD,
BUT I GOT
TO SEE
ALL THE
COOL BANDS.

GETTING OLD IS LIKE CLIMBING A MOUNTAIN; YOU GET A LITTLE OUT OF BREATH, BUT THE VIEW IS MUCH BETTER!

INGRID BERGMAN

WE DON'T GROW OLDER, WE GROW RIPER.

PABLO PICASSO

ONE SHOULD NEVER MAKE ONE'S DEBUT WITH A SCANDAL. ONE SHOULD RESERVE THAT TO GIVE INTEREST TO ONE'S OLD AGE.

OSCAR WILDE

IF I'D KNOWN I WAS GOING TO LIVE THIS LONG, I'D HAVE TAKEN BETTER CARE OF MYSELF.

EUBIE BLAKE

THERE'S NEVER ENOUGH TIME TO DO ALL THE NOTHING YOU WANT.

BILL WATTERSON

I ADMIRE THOSE PEOPLE WHO HOLD ON TO THEIR ELEGANCE IN OLD AGE BUT I'D RATHER HAVE FUN.

HEATHER GRAHAM

AGE IS A HIGH PRICE TO PAY FOR MATURITY.

TOM STOPPARD

GETTING OLDER IS NO PROBLEM. YOU JUST HAVE TO LIVE LONG ENOUGH.

GROUCHO MARX

WHEN YOU ARE DISSATISFIED AND WOULD LIKE TO GO BACK TO YOUTH, THINK OF ALGEBRA.

OLD AGE ISN'T SO BAD WHEN YOU CONSIDER THE ALTERNATIVE.

MAURICE CHEVALIER

BE ECCENTRIC *NOW.*
DON'T WAIT FOR OLD AGE TO WEAR PURPLE.

REGINA BRETT

STARTING TO THINK I'LL NEVER BE OLD ENOUGH TO KNOW BETTER.

MY GRANDMOTHER STARTED WALKING FIVE MILES A DAY WHEN SHE WAS SIXTY. SHE'S NINETY-SEVEN NOW, AND WE DON'T KNOW WHERE THE HELL SHE IS.

ELLEN DEGENERES

THE OLDER I GROW, THE MORE I DISTRUST THE FAMILIAR DOCTRINE THAT AGE BRINGS WISDOM.

H. L. MENCKEN

YOU CAN'T HELP GETTING OLDER, BUT YOU DON'T HAVE TO GET OLD.

GEORGE BURNS

I LOVE
EVERYTHING THAT'S OLD: OLD FRIENDS, OLD TIMES, OLD MANNERS, OLD BOOKS, OLD WINE.
OLIVER GOLDSMITH

ONE ADVANTAGE OF GETTING OLD: LESS AND LESS PEER PRESSURE.

TO ME, OLD AGE IS ALWAYS FIFTEEN YEARS OLDER THAN I AM.

BERNARD BARUCH

YOU ARE ONLY YOUNG ONCE, BUT YOU CAN STAY IMMATURE INDEFINITELY.

AS SOON AS YOU FEEL TOO OLD TO DO A THING, *DO IT.*

MARGARET DELAND

GRANT ME THE SENILITY TO FORGET THE PEOPLE I NEVER LIKED, THE GOOD FORTUNE TO RUN INTO THE ONES I DO, AND THE EYESIGHT TO TELL THE DIFFERENCE.

AND SO THE ADVENTURE BEGINS.